EASY PIANO

Classical Music
FOR A CLASSIC WEDDING

ISBN 978-0-634-02599-0

HAL•LEONARD®
CORPORATION
7777 W. BLUEMOUND RD. P.O. BOX 13819 MILWAUKEE, WI 53213

For all works contained herein:
Unauthorized copying, arranging, adapting, recording or public performance is an infringement of copyright.
Infringers are liable under the law.

Visit Hal Leonard Online at
www.halleonard.com

CONTENTS

AIR ON THE G STRING
from ORCHESTRAL SUITE NO. 3

By JOHANN SEBASTIAN BACH

Slowly and stately

Copyright © 1999 by HAL LEONARD CORPORATION
International Copyright Secured   All Rights Reserved

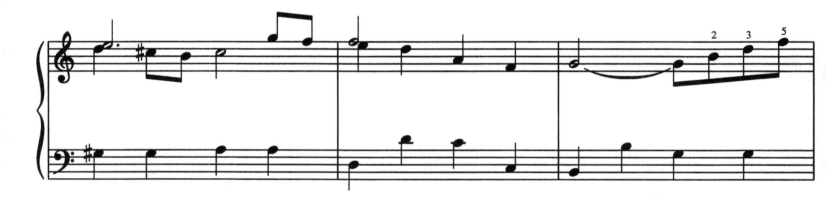

ALLEGRO MAESTOSO
from WATER MUSIC

By GEORGE FRIDERIC HANDEL

Allegro maestoso (stately, with movement)

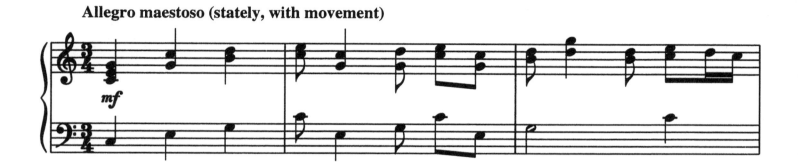

Copyright © 1999 by HAL LEONARD CORPORATION
International Copyright Secured   All Rights Reserved

AVE MARIA

By FRANZ SCHUBERT

Very Slowly

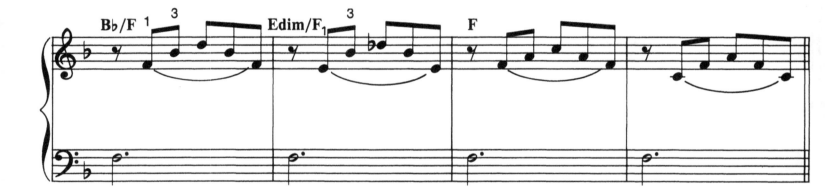

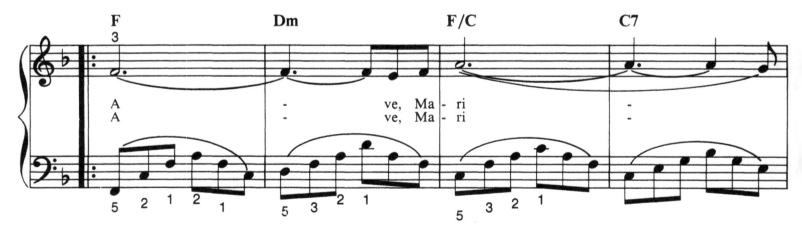

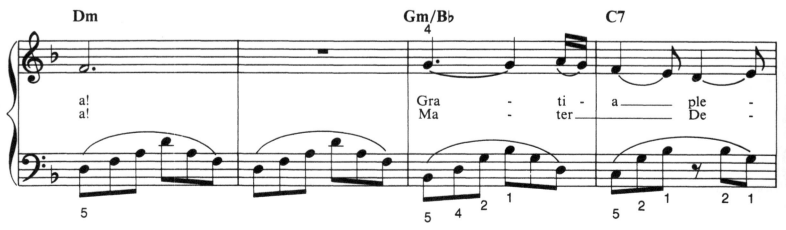

Copyright © 1985 by HAL LEONARD CORPORATION
International Copyright Secured   All Rights Reserved

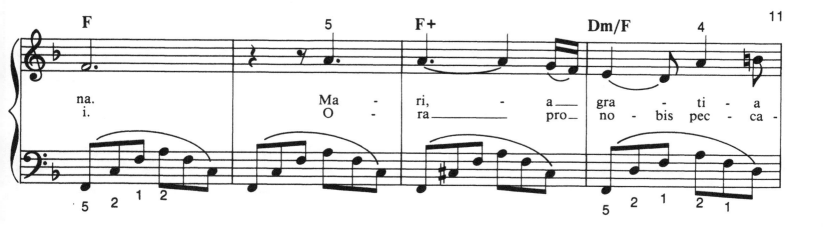

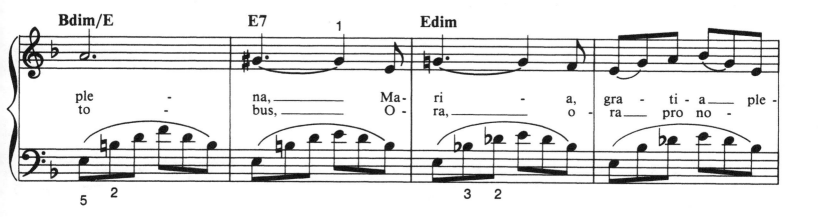

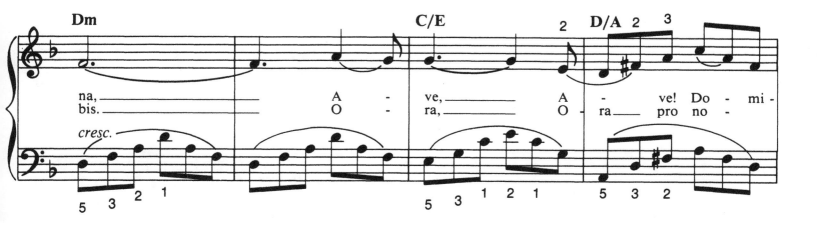

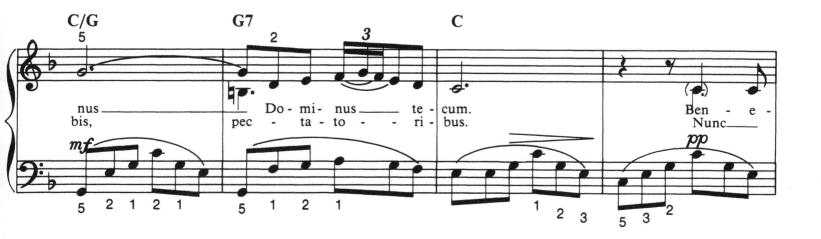

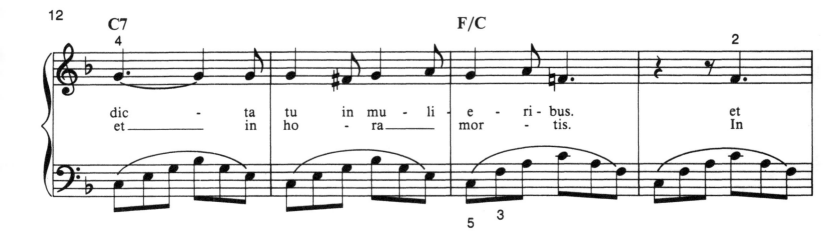

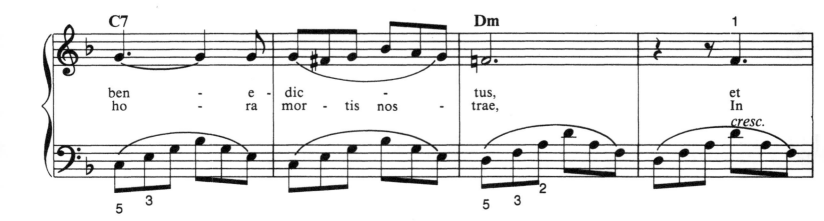

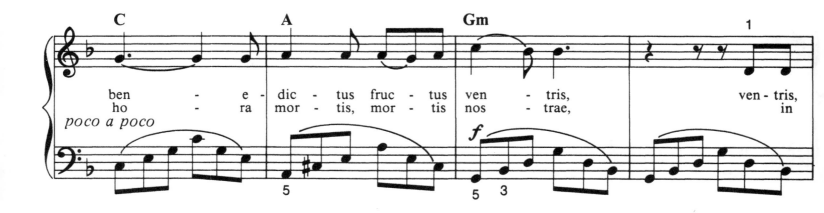

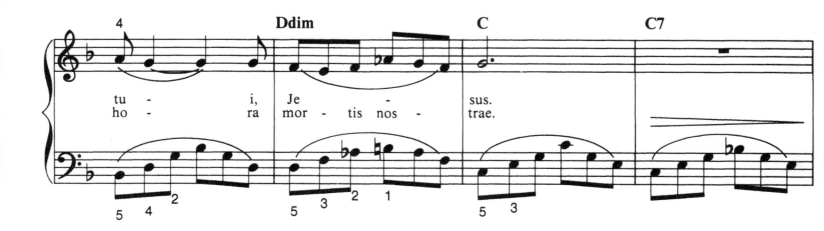

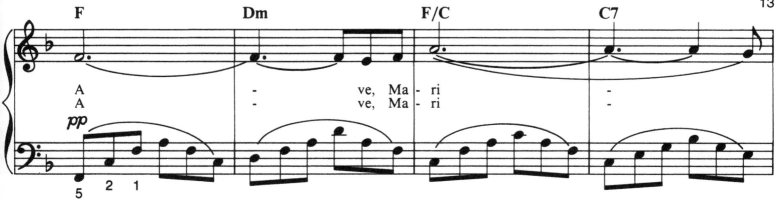

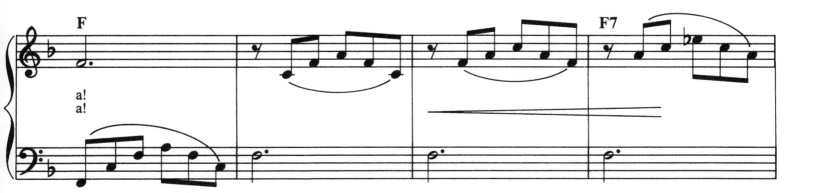

2nd time to Coda

CODA

AVE MARIA

based on Prelude in C Major by J.S. Bach

By CHARLES GOUNOD

Slowly, with reverence

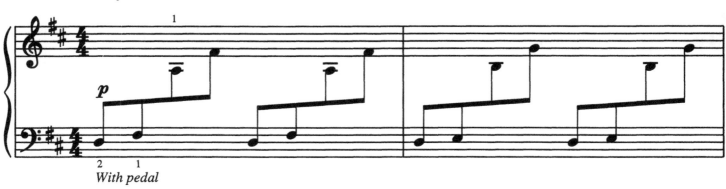

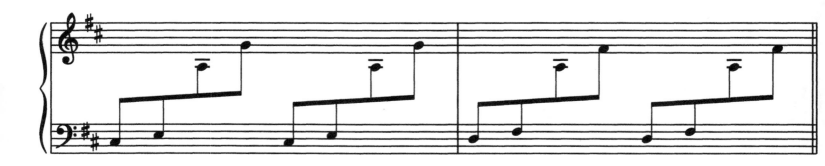

A - ve Ma - ri -

a, gra - ti - a

Copyright © 1996 by HAL LEONARD CORPORATION
International Copyright Secured   All Rights Reserved

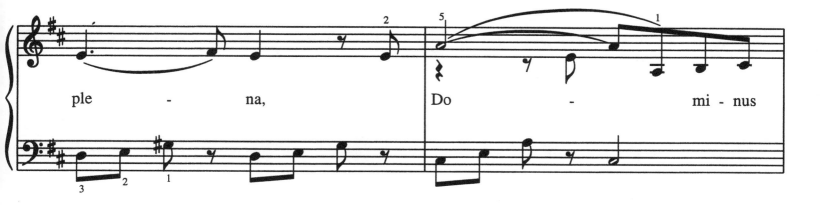

ple - na, Do - mi - nus

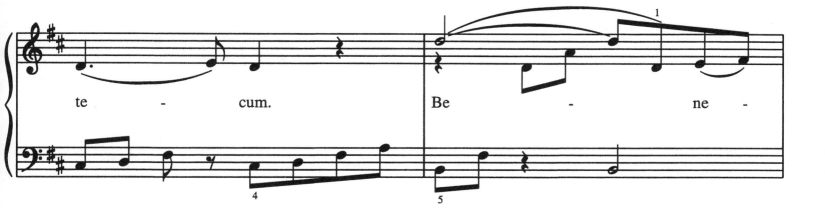

te - cum. Be - ne -

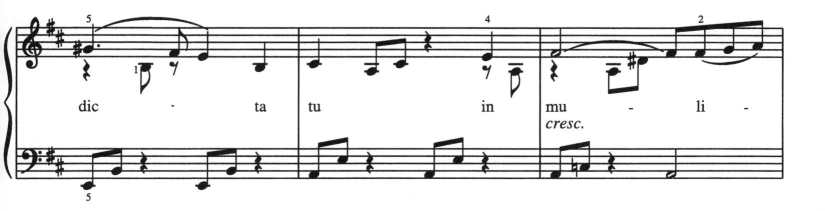

dic - ta tu in mu - li -

cresc.

e - ri - bus et _____ be - ne - dic - tus

fruc - tus ____ ven - tris ____

tu - i Je - sus. Sanc - ta Ma -

ri - a, sanc - ta Ma -

ri - a, Ma - ri - a, o - ra __ pro

no - bis, no - bis pec-ca - to - ri-bus,

nunc _____ et _ in ho - ra, in ho - ra ___

mor - tis _ nos - trae, _ A - men!

A - men!

BIST DU BEI MIR

(Be Thou with Me)

By JOHANN SEBASTIAN BACH

Moderately

mp

With pedal

p   cresc.

mf

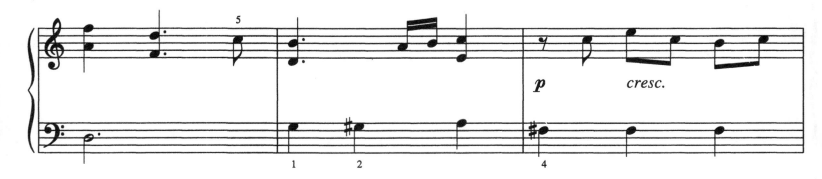

p   cresc.

Copyright © 2001 by HAL LEONARD CORPORATION
International Copyright Secured   All Rights Reserved

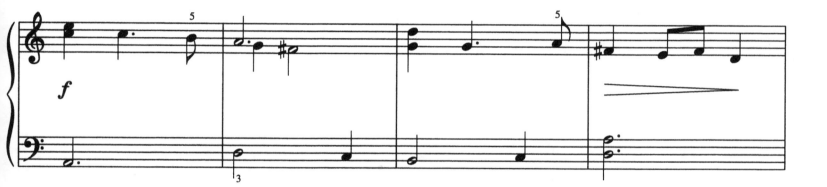

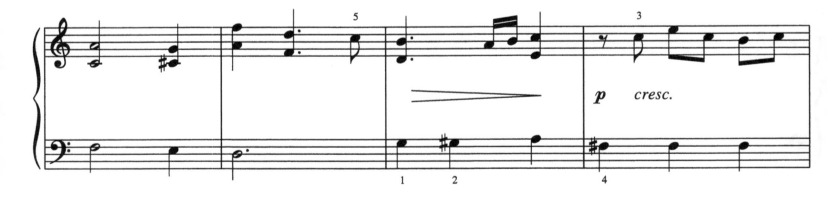

BRIDAL CHORUS
from the opera LOHENGRIN

By RICHARD WAGNER

Moderately

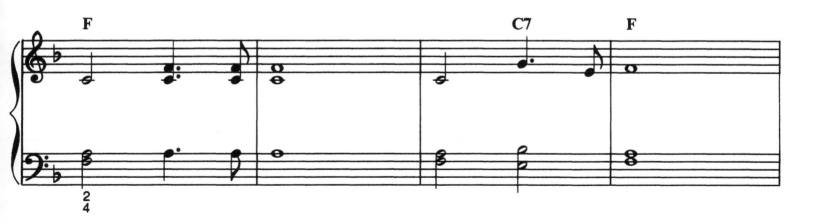

Copyright © 1985 by HAL LEONARD CORPORATION
International Copyright Secured   All Rights Reserved

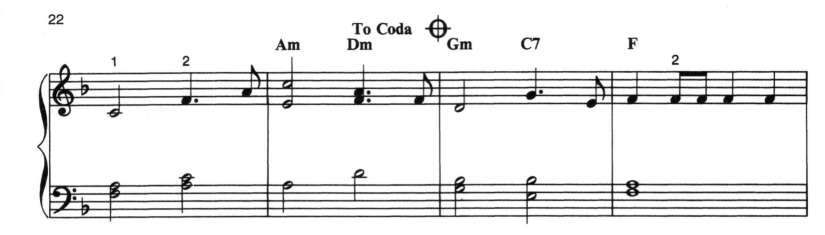

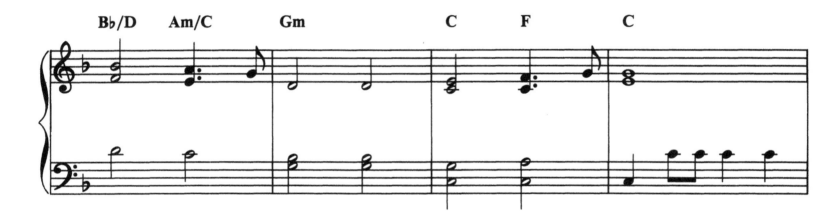

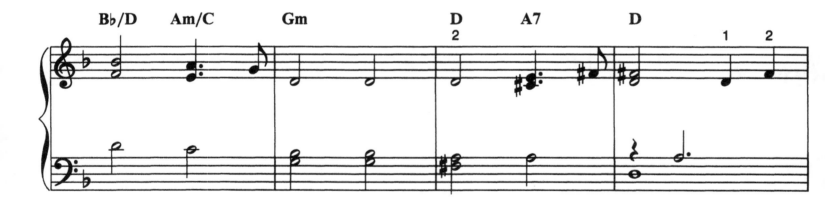

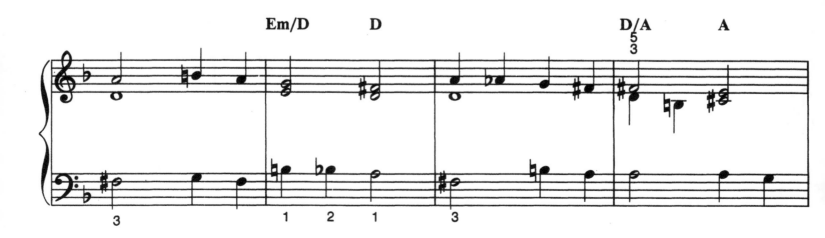

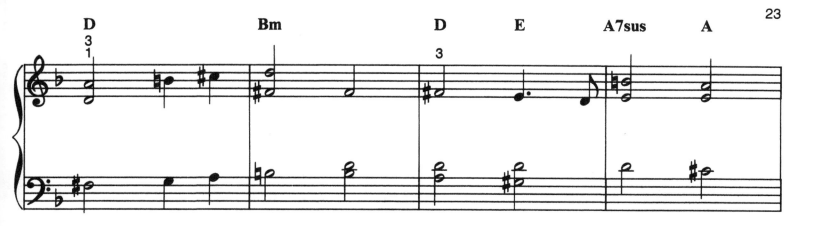

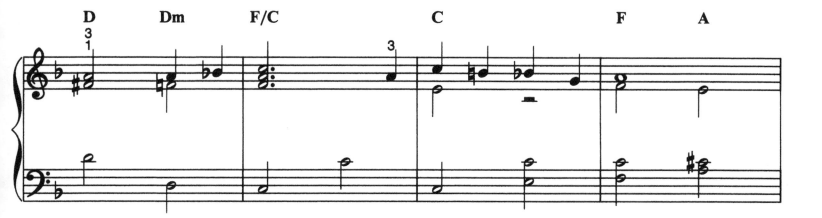

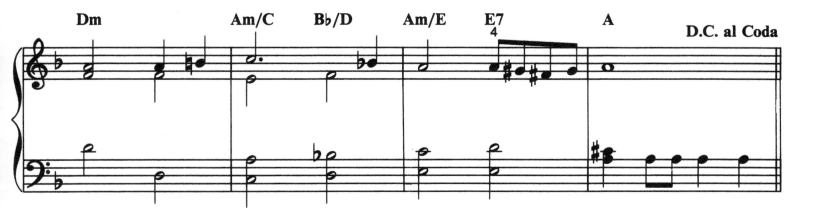

CANON IN D MAJOR

By JOHANN PACHELBEL

Copyright © 1999 by HAL LEONARD CORPORATION
International Copyright Secured   All Rights Reserved

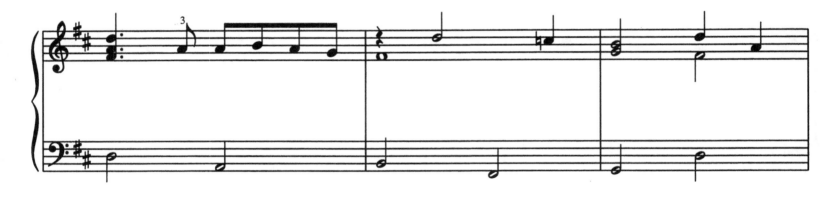

LA CANZONE DI DORETTA
(Chi bel sogno di Doretta)
from LA RONDINE

Words and Music by
GIACOMO PUCCINI

Slowly

Moderately

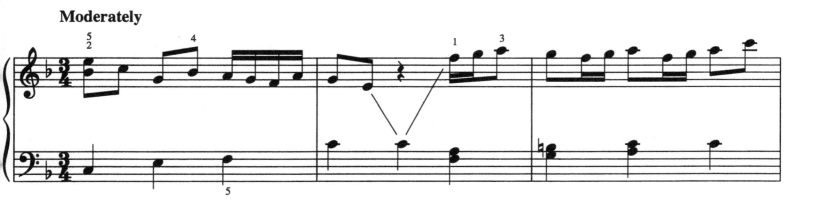

Copyright © 2001 by HAL LEONARD CORPORATION
International Copyright Secured   All Rights Reserved

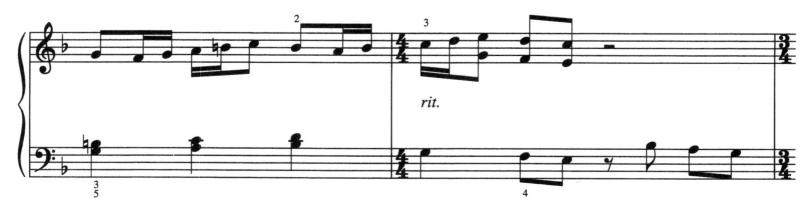

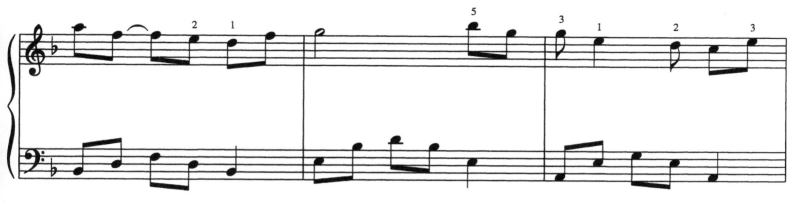

DU RING AN MEINEM FINGER

By ROBERT SCHUMANN

Moderately

Copyright © 2001 by HAL LEONARD CORPORATION
International Copyright Secured   All Rights Reserved

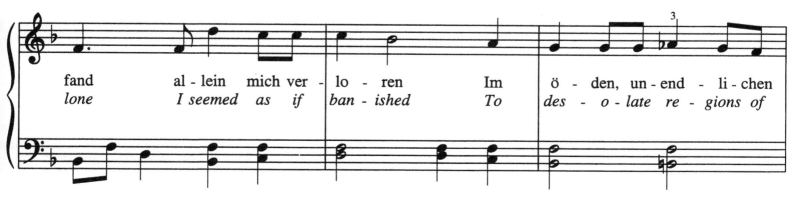

fand al - lein mich ver - lo - ren Im
lone I seemed as if ban - ished To
ö - den, un - end - li - chen
des - o - late re - gions of

Raum. Du __ Ring an mei - nem Fin - ger, Da __
night. The __ ring up - on my fin - ger, Has __

hast du mich erst be - lehrt, Hast __ mei - nem Blick er -
giv - en glad thoughts a birth, For - bid - den clouds to

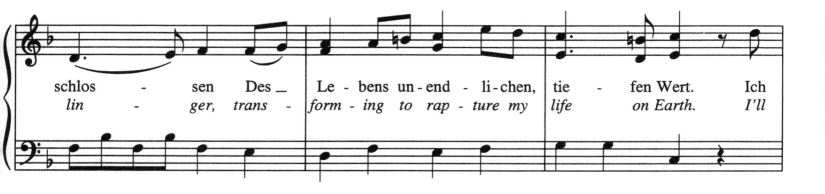

schlos - sen Des __ Le - bens un - end - li - chen, tie - fen Wert. Ich
lin - ger, trans - form - ing to rap - ture my life on Earth. I'll

will ihm die - nen, ihm le - ben, Ihm
live for him, _____ be - long to him, Ihm trans -

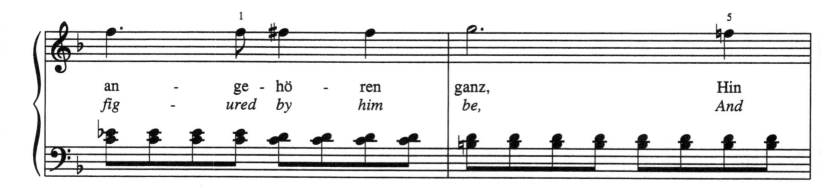

an - ge - hö - ren ganz, Hin
fig - ured by him be, And

sel - ber mich ge - ben und fin - den ver - klärt mich, und
give ___ of my - self so that we'll ev - er be, mich, you and

fin - den ver - klärt mich in sei - nem Glanz. Du ___ Ring an mei - nem
I be - come one and re - sult ___ in we. The ___ ring up - on my

Fin - ger, Mein___ gol - de - nes Rin - ge -
fin - ger, My___ beau - ti - ful ring of

lein, Ich___ drü - cke dich fromm an die Lip - pen, Dich
gold, My___ lips on you fer - vent - ly lin - ger, As

fromm an die Lip-pen, an das Her - ze mein.
close to my lips, ___ to my heart I hold.

ENTREAT ME NOT TO LEAVE THEE
(Song of Ruth)

Words and Music by
CHARLES GOUNOD

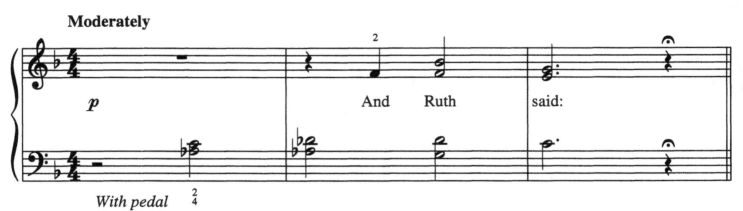

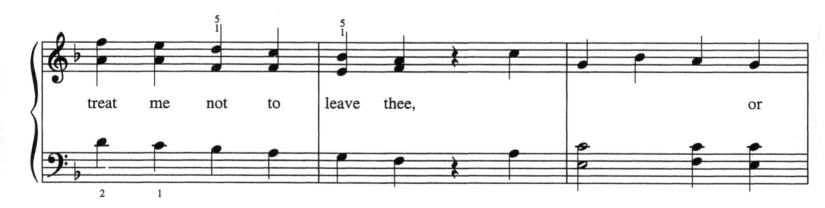

Copyright © 2001 by HAL LEONARD CORPORATION
International Copyright Secured All Rights Reserved

whith-er thou go - est   I will go, and   where thou lodg - est

I will lodge;   whith-er thou go - est   I ____ will go, and

cresc.

where thou lodg - est ____   I will lodge,   where thou lodg - est,

dim.   *p*

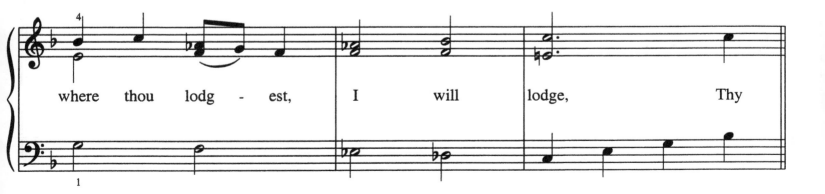

where thou lodg - est,   I will   lodge,   Thy

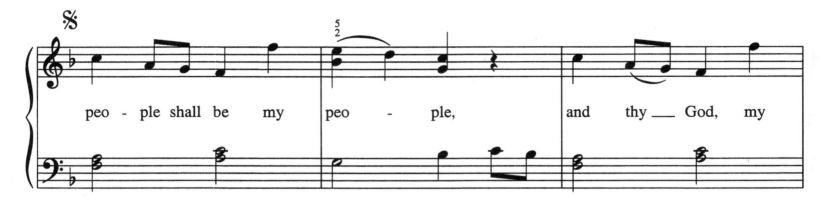

peo - ple shall be my peo - ple, and thy ___ God, my

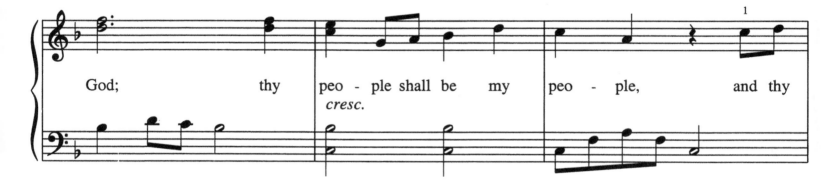

God; thy peo - ple shall be my peo - ple, and thy

cresc.

God, my God; Thy peo - ple shall be my

f

Fine

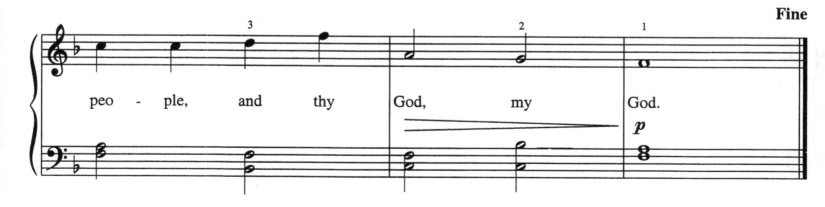

peo - ple, and thy God, my God.

p

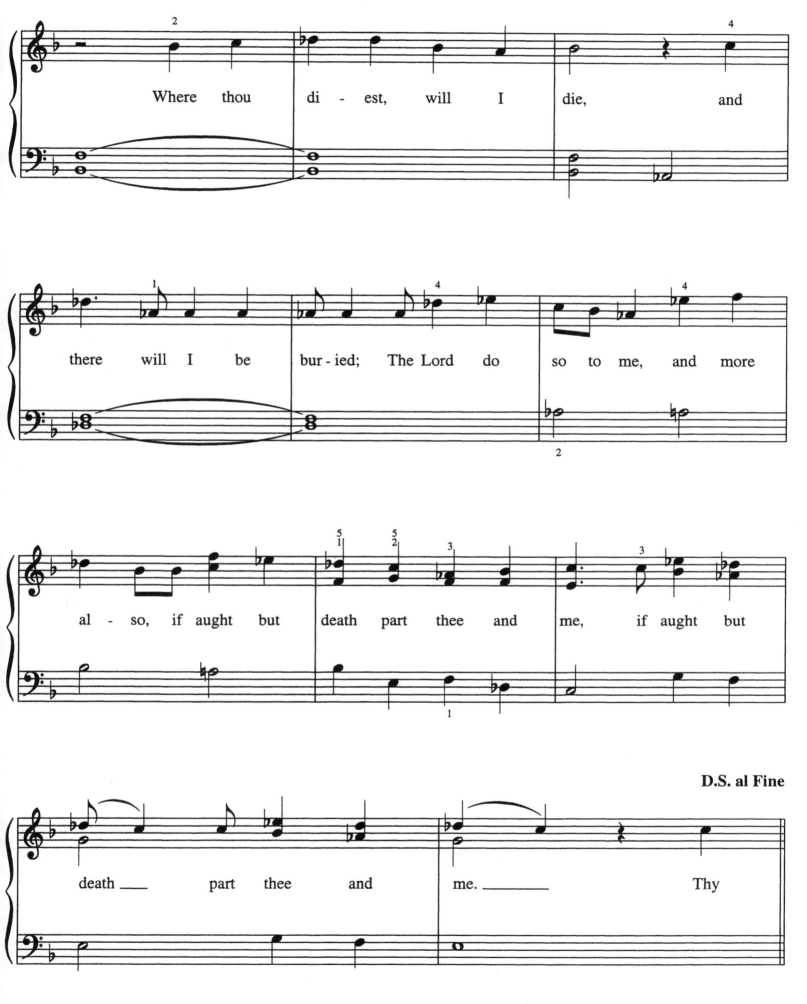

HORNPIPE
from WATER MUSIC

By GEORGE FRIDERIC HANDEL

With energy

mf

With pedal

Copyright © 2001 by HAL LEONARD CORPORATION
International Copyright Secured   All Rights Reserved

ICH LIEBE DICH
(I Love You)

Words and Music by
EDVARD GRIEG

Moderately

Copyright © 2001 by HAL LEONARD CORPORATION
International Copyright Secured   All Rights Reserved

lie - be dich in Zeit und E - wig - keit! Ich lie - be dich in Zeit und
all of time and of e - ter - ni - ty, For all of time and of e -

E - wig - keit!
ter - ni - ty!

Ich den - ke dein, kann stets nur dei - ner den - ken,
Your thoughts are mine and I think of you on - ly,

Nur dei - nem Gluck ist die - ses Herz ge - weiht;
Pledg - ing my heart to bring you hap - pi - ness;

Wie Gott auch mag des Le - bens Schick-sal
What - ev - er God has des -tined life to

len - ken, Ich lie - be dich, ich lie - be dich, ich
show me, I love ___ you, I love ___ you! ich

lie - be dich in Zeit und E - wig-keit! Ich lie - be dich in Zeit und
all of time and of e - ter - ni - ty, For all of time and of e -

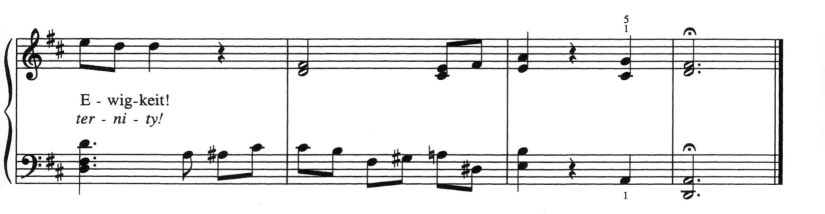

E - wig-keit!
ter - ni - ty!

JESU, JOY OF MAN'S DESIRING

By JOHANN SEBASTIAN BACH

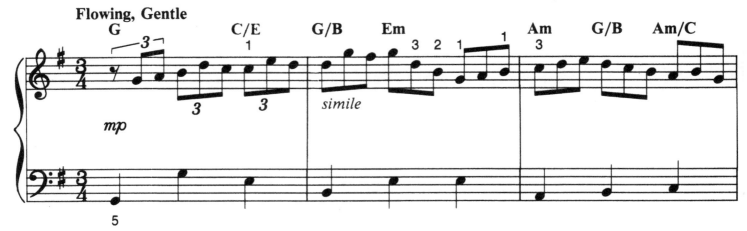

Je - su,
Through - the

joy   of   man's   de - sir - ing.
way where hope   is   guid - ing,

Copyright © 1985 by HAL LEONARD CORPORATION
International Copyright Secured   All Rights Reserved

Ho - ly wis - dom, love___ most___ bright.
Hark, what peace - ful mus - ic___ rings.

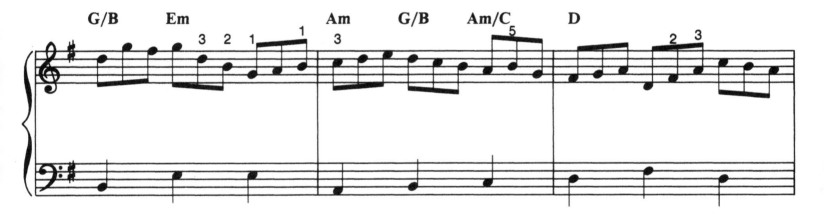

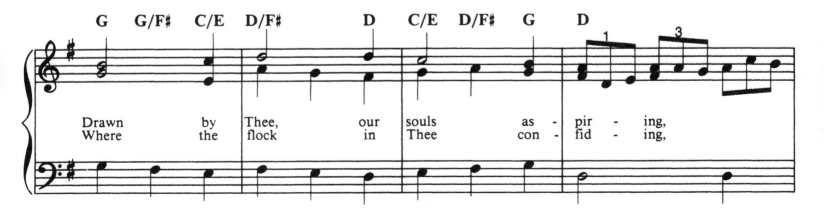

Drawn by Thee, our souls as - pir - ing,
Where the flock in Thee con - fid - ing,

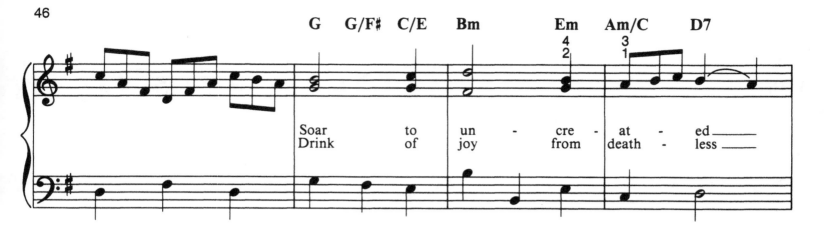

Soar to un - cre - at - ed
Drink of joy from death - less

light.
springs.

Word of God our
Theirs is beau - ty's

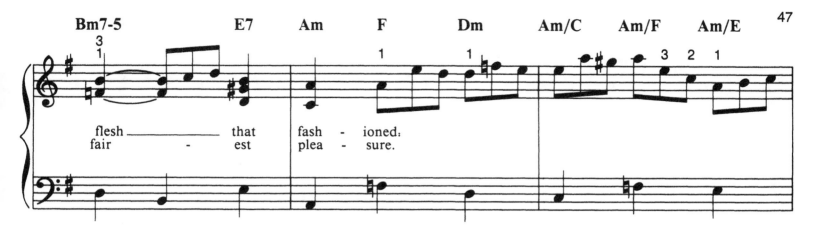

flesh _____ that fash - ioned:
fair - est plea - sure.

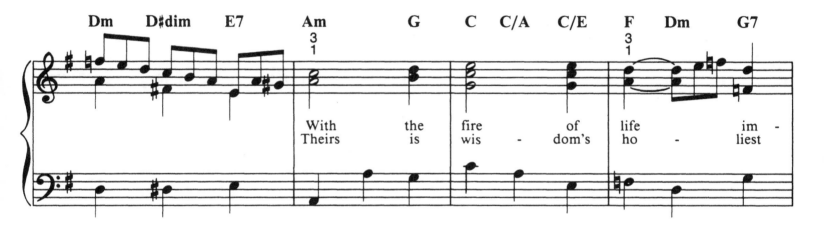

With the fire of life im -
Theirs is wis - dom's ho - liest

pas - sioned.
trea - sure.

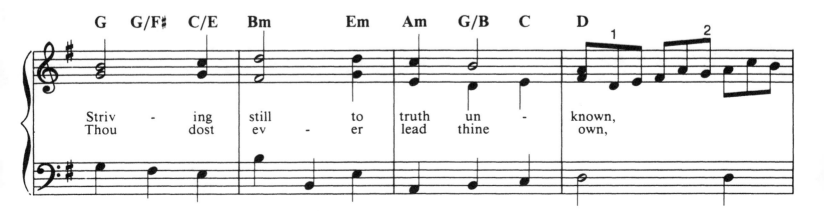

Striv - ing still to truth un - known,
Thou dost ev - er lead thine own,

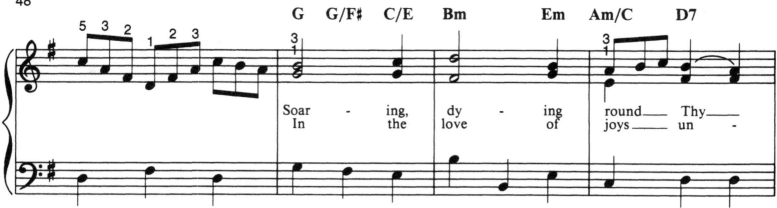

Soar - ing, dy - ing round___ Thy___
In - the love - of joys___ un -

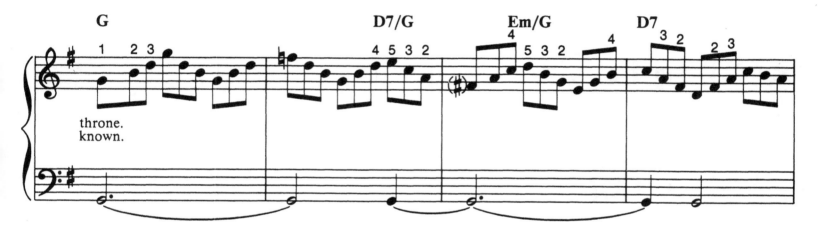

throne.
known.

poco ritard.

NIMROD
from ENIGMA VARIATIONS

By EDWARD ELGAR

Slowly

p

With pedal

Copyright © 2001 by HAL LEONARD CORPORATION
International Copyright Secured   All Rights Reserved

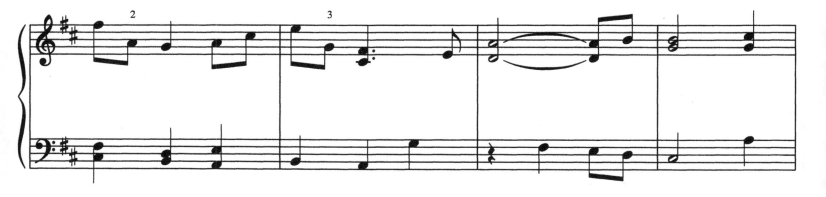

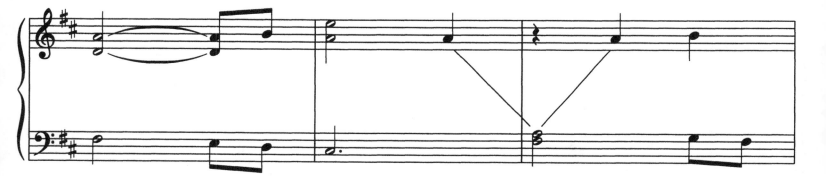

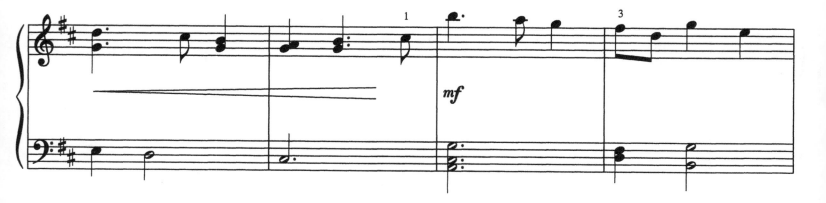

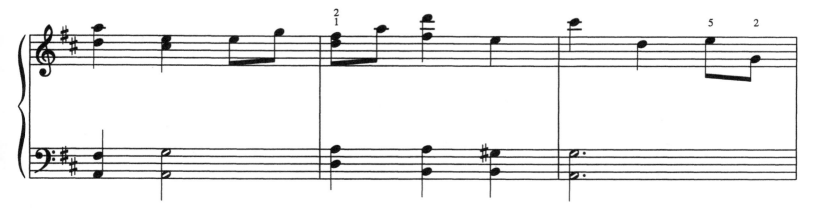

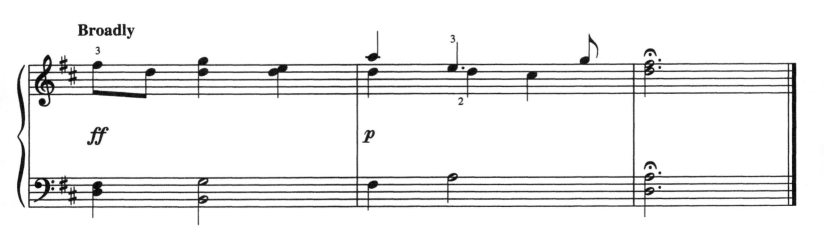

JUPITER
from THE PLANETS

By GUSTAV HOLST

Moderately

mf

With pedal

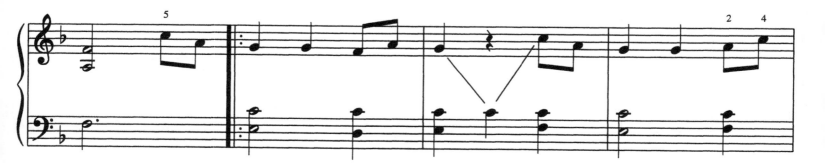

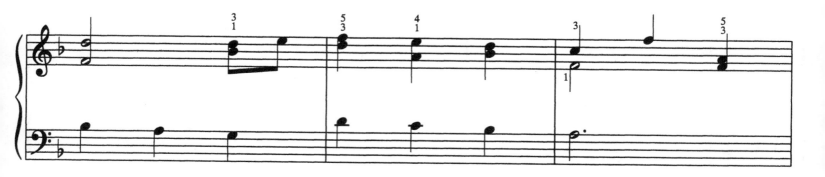

Copyright © 2001 by HAL LEONARD CORPORATION
International Copyright Secured   All Rights Reserved

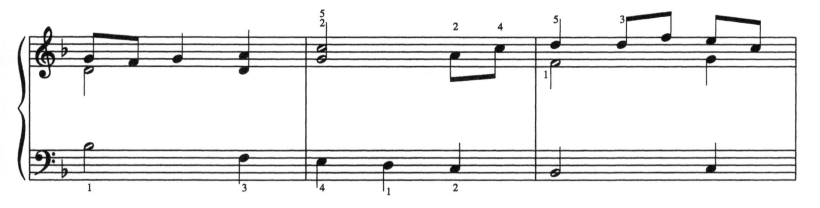

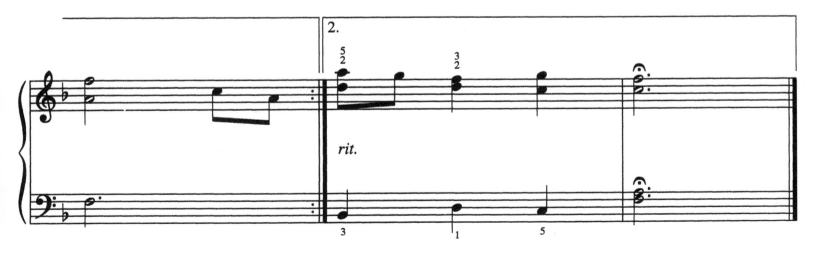

LARGO
from the opera XERXES

By GEORGE FRIDERIC HANDEL

Slowly and solemnly

With pedal

Copyright © 1999 by HAL LEONARD CORPORATION
International Copyright Secured   All Rights Reserved

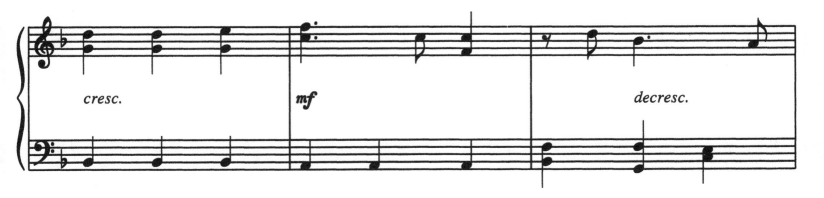

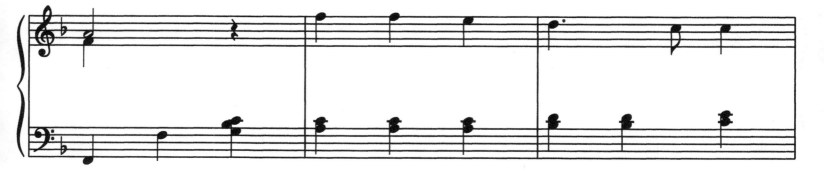

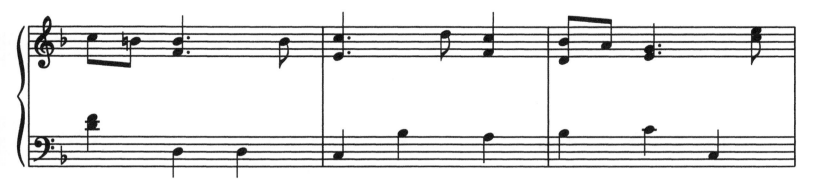

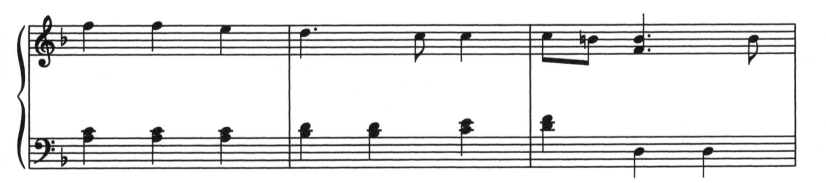

MEDITATION
from THAÏS

By JULES MASSENET

Moderately slow

With pedal

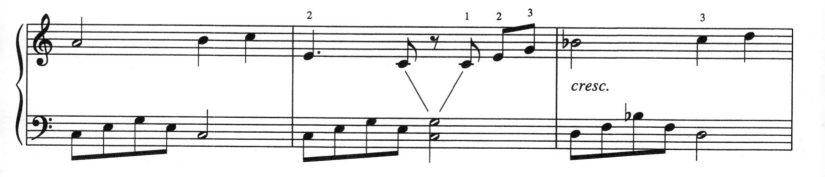

Copyright © 2001 by HAL LEONARD CORPORATION
International Copyright Secured   All Rights Reserved

To Coda $\bigoplus$

A little faster

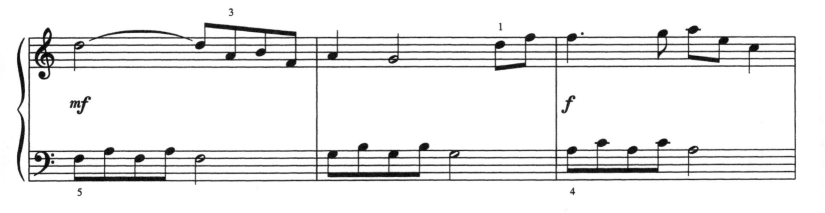

Calmly

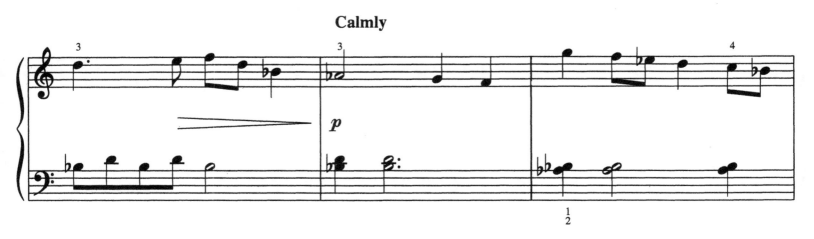

D.C. al Coda

CODA

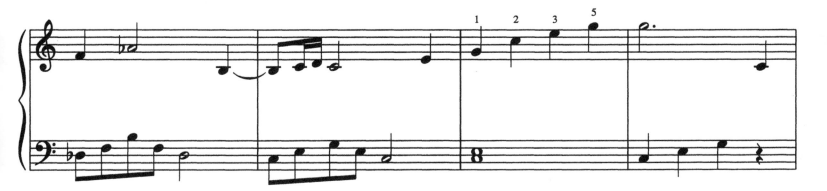

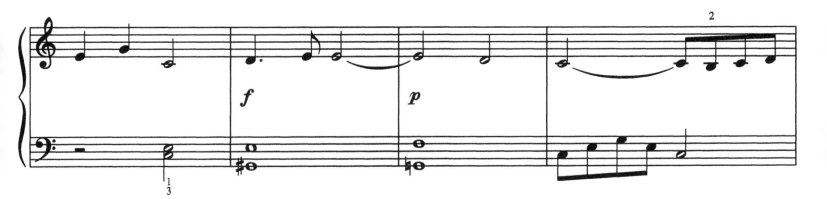

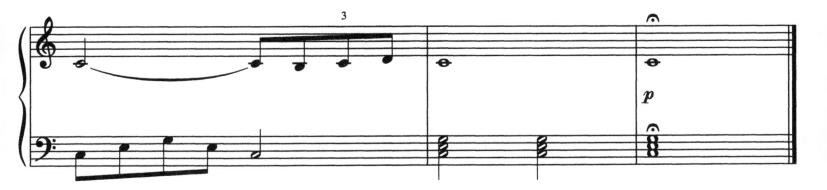

ODE TO JOY
from SYMPHONY NO. 9 in D Minor
Fourth Movement Choral Theme

Music by LUDWIG VAN BEETHOVEN

Copyright © 1983 by HAL LEONARD CORPORATION
International Copyright Secured   All Rights Reserved

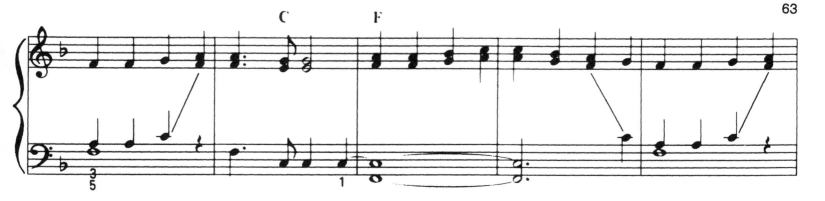

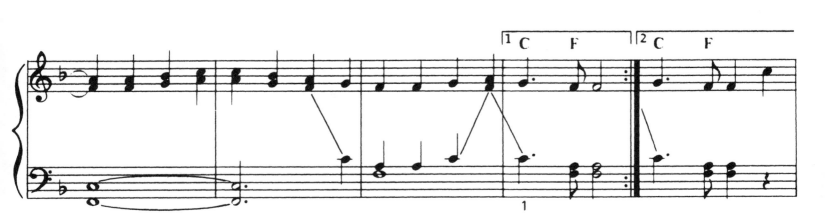

PANIS ANGELICUS
(Oh Lord Most Holy)

By CÉSAR FRANCK

Slowly

Copyright © 1999 by HAL LEONARD CORPORATION
International Copyright Secured   All Rights Reserved

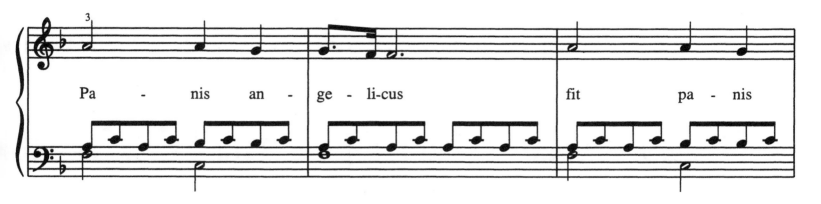

Pa - nis an - ge - li-cus fit pa - nis

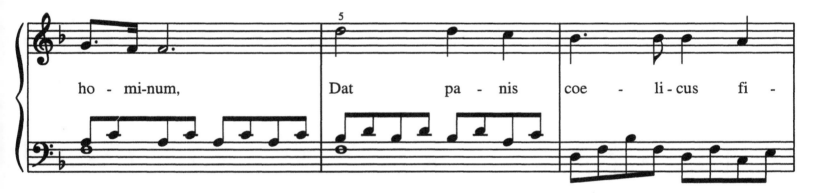

ho - mi-num, Dat pa - nis coe - li-cus fi -

gu - ris ter - mi - num. O res mi -

ra - bi-lis man - du - cat Do - mi-num,

Pau - per, pau - per, ser - vus et hum - mi -

lis, Pau - per, pau - per,

ser - vus et hum - mi - lis.

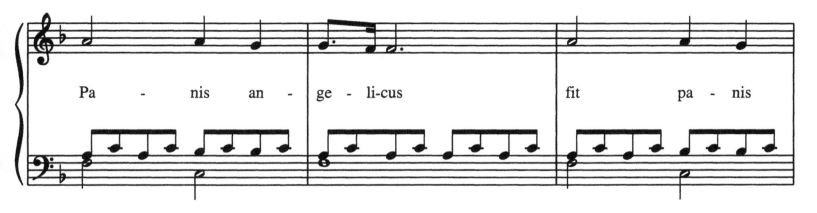

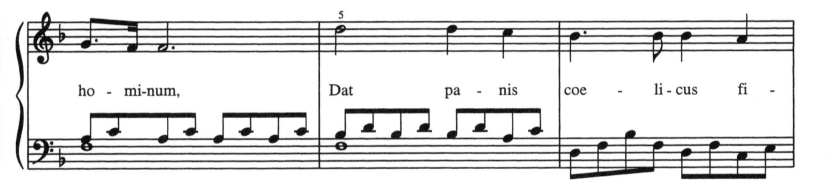

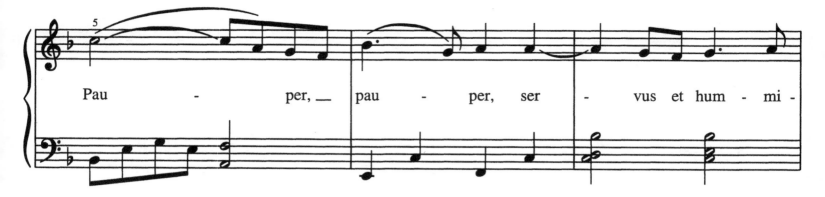

Pau - per, __ pau - per, ser - vus et hum - mi -

lis, Pau - per, __ pau - per ser -

- vus, __ ser - vus et hum - mi - lis.

RONDEAU

By JEAN-JOSEPH MOURET

Copyright © 1999 by HAL LEONARD CORPORATION
International Copyright Secured   All Rights Reserved

SHEEP MAY SAFELY GRAZE

from CANTATA 208

By JOHANN SEBASTIAN BACH

Andante

Copyright © 1999 by HAL LEONARD CORPORATION
International Copyright Secured   All Rights Reserved

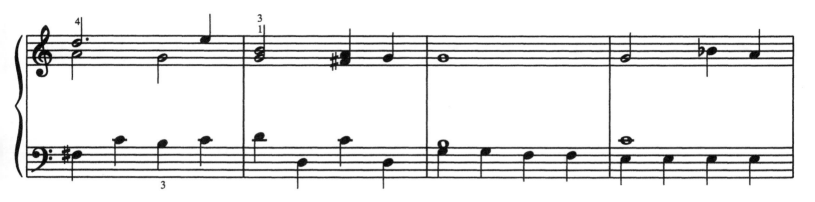

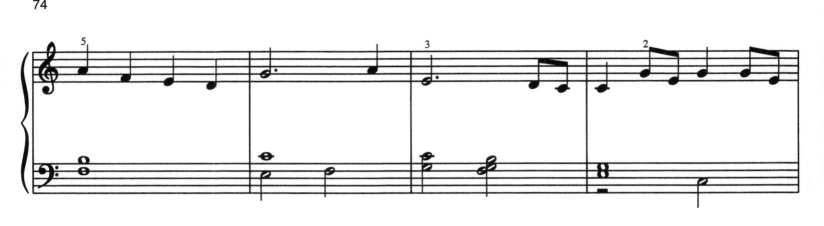

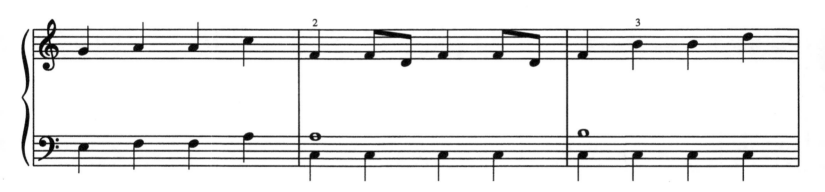

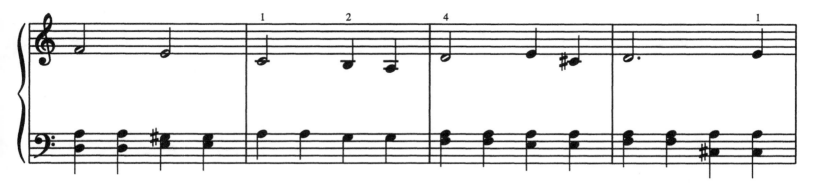

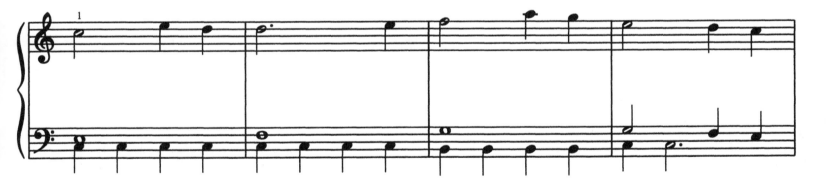

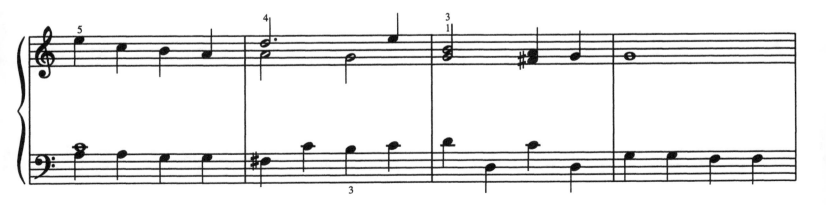

TRUMPET TUNE

By HENRY PURCELL

Stately (♩ = 1 count)

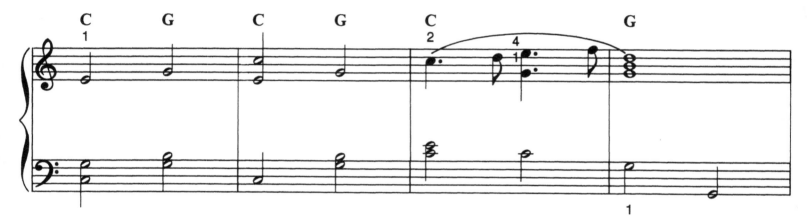

Copyright © 1985 by HAL LEONARD CORPORATION
International Copyright Secured   All Rights Reserved

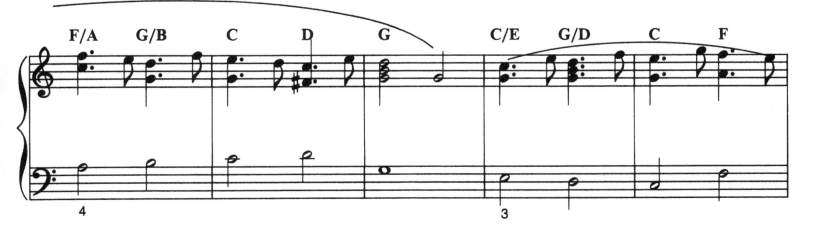

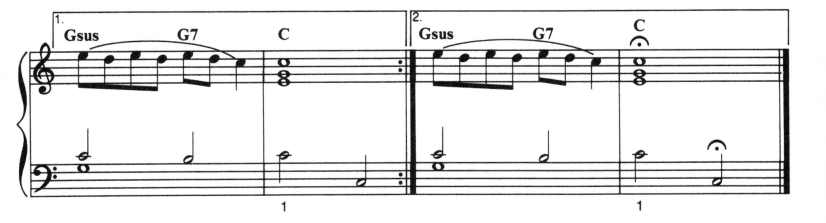

TRUMPET VOLUNTARY

By JEREMIAH CLARKE

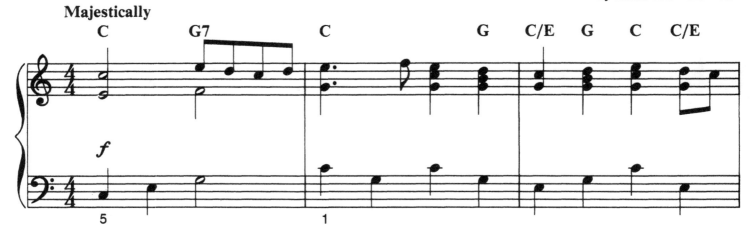

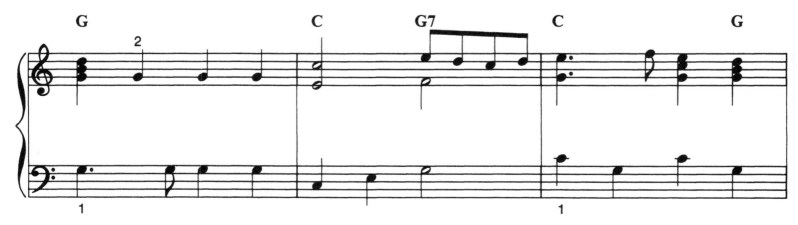

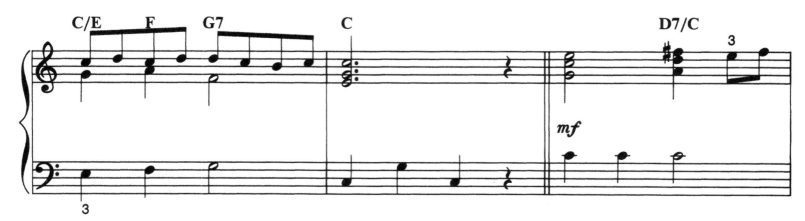

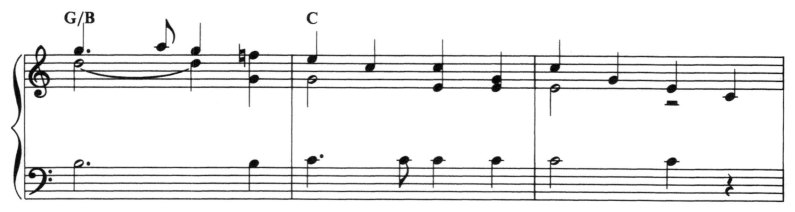

Copyright © 1985 by HAL LEONARD CORPORATION
International Copyright Secured   All Rights Reserved

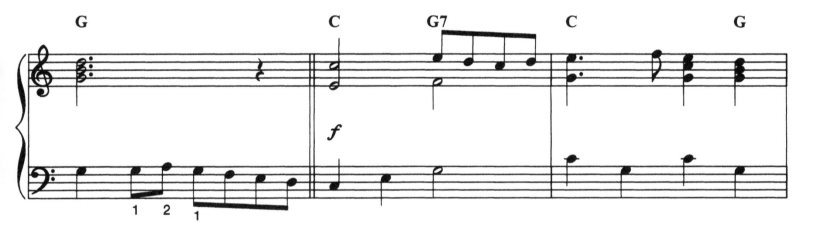

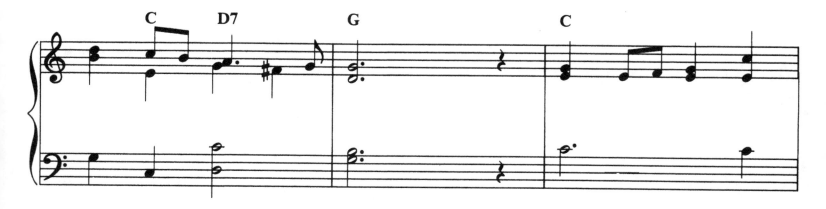

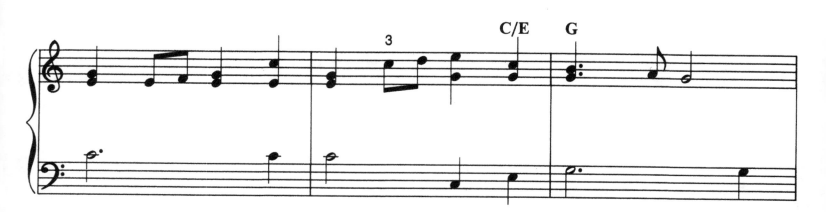

WEDDING MARCH
from A MIDSUMMER NIGHT'S DREAM

By FELIX MENDELSSOHN

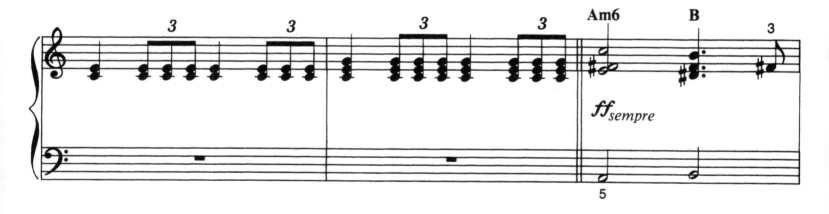

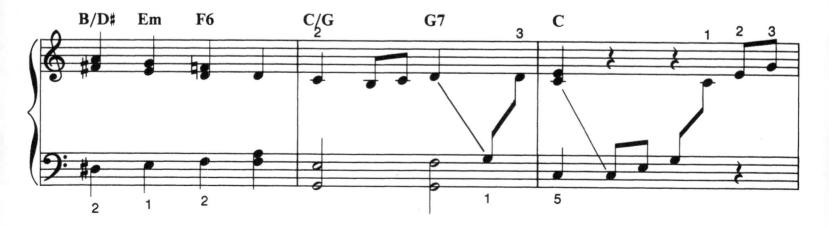

Copyright © 1985 by HAL LEONARD CORPORATION
International Copyright Secured   All Rights Reserved

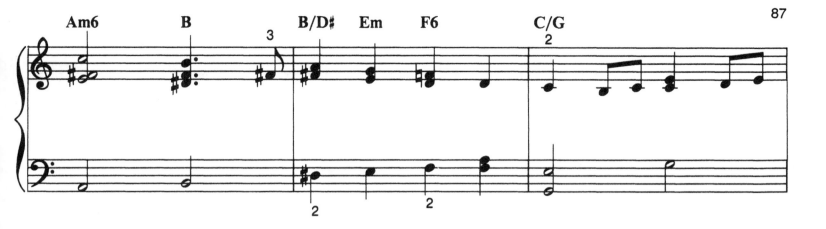

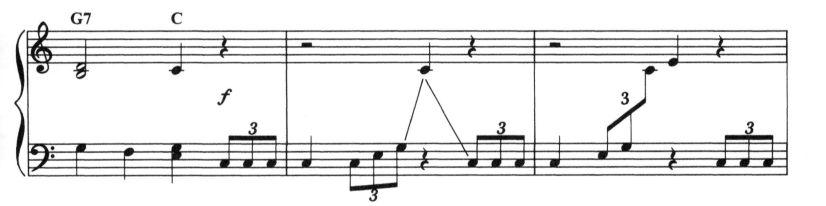

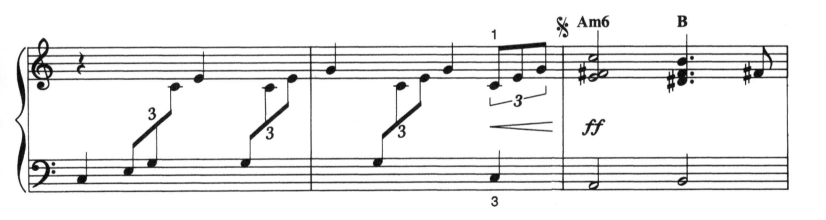

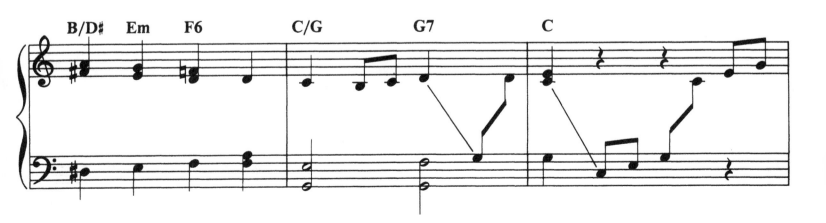